I0441082

The Lonely Scum Thinks Alone

Jacob Tobias

Copyright © 2013 by Jacob Tobias

All rights reserved.

Book design and editing by Jacob Tobias using Lulu.com
Cover design by Jacob Tobias using Lulu.com

No part of this book may be reproduced in any form or by any electronic or mechanical means including information storage and retrieval systems, without permission in writing from the author.

Jacob Tobias
www.facebook.com/ImNotScouse
Twitter @FizzyGingerBeer

First Printing: October 2013
Lulu.com

ISBN 978-1-291-59774-5

Thanks To

Anyone who was ever there

To everyone who wasn't, then you know what you can do

Top of the Pops Magazine for keeping me sane

Bethan, Lee, Tracey, Heather, Katie

For pulling me out of the deepest and darkest waters

Contents

The Lonely Scum Thinks Alone

I was 14 when I started writing lyrics. Most of them were songs in my head. Most of the lyrics in this book weren't. They were different.

During 1999 I started getting bullied even more than usual, and ended up writing ranting, angry, confused lyrics. I kept these lyrics separate from the rest of them and only recently re- read them.

They weren't easy to read and even less so to put them into a book.

I'm still not sure why I have...

Jacob Tobias

1. Here

Here in a room
Facing my doom
If I'm not talked to soon
I'll be sitting in gloom
Watching the moon
And humming a tune

Here in a school
With dreadful rules
People stare and drool
Making me look a fool
Sitting in a science room
On an old wooden stool

Here in a bed
Cuddled up with a ted
Rather have a person instead
In my little bed
My body feels like lead
I better lay down my head

Here at night
Ghosts give me a fright
I hold my teddy tight
Turn on the light
Then with all my might
I try to sleep tight
Goodnight

2. What's The Point?

What's the point of me being here
When all I am is a dirty queer

What's the point of me living every day
When all I do is listen and obey

What's the point of me trying
When I only end up crying

What's the point of being alive
When all I do is crouch and hide

What's the point of me trying to make amends
When I still won't have any friends

What's the point of being beaten about
When I know I only have to shout

What's the point of me going to school
When I have to obey the other kids rules

What's the point of always trying to explain
When I'm going to be made to live a life of shame

What's the point of me picking up the phone
I'm still gonna be here all alone

What's the point of me trying to get through all this
Everyone's still gonna take the piss

What's the point of me running away
I'm still gonna have to come back one day

What's the point of living a lie
I might as well curl up and die

What's the point of me going through life

With all it's trouble and strife

What's the point of me taking a girl to bed
When I'd rather have Andrew Lee-Potts instead

What's the point of me trying to be tough
When everyone says I'm a puff

What's the point of me trying to be free
When nobody wants me to be

THE END

3. Someday

Someday I'll probably find myself around people who won't want to hurt me.
People that actually care a little bit about me.

Someday people will probably make me happy at Christmas, a time of the year when people are usually nice to each other, everyone is normally full of life and happiness at Christmas.

I can remember times like that, nobody bothers with me no more, even the teachers take notice of everyone else and they always leave me out of things.

Everyone decides to make it a really miserable time of the year by telling me that I'm unnatural, sick and mentally ill.

I even get hit a lot more often and harder.

Birthdays aren't much different, everyone remembers everyone else's, but never mine, even though some people know when it is.

Everyone's birthday is written down in the register and the teachers seem to notice them all except mine. It's only ever been mentioned once and that was in the first year.

The form tutor went through everyone's birthday in order one day and when they'd finished I realised mine hadn't been read out.

Even relatives don't visit on birthdays anymore.

4. Why Bother?

Why bother going through each day, getting hit and skitted and almost beaten to death by a load of queer bashers who think I won't tell anyone because I'm afraid they'll find out the truth…..
They're right, I am afraid.

Why bother getting changed into clean clothes every day, I mean, I'm not going anywhere am I? It's not worth getting changed every single day when no one bothers to come near you anymore. Apart from the journey to school, I only leave the house once a week.

Why bother eating food every day if you're not going to use up it's energy. Even if I lose weight, it won't do any harm, no one would notice anyway. So I just sit there stuffing my face with chocolate and crisps and loads of junk food.

Why bother to be nice to people when they're not nice to you.
My mum expects me to write a birthday card to somebody who used to hang around with me, well he can forget it. If he ignores my existence, then I can't be expected to pretend everything's alright can I?
So I'll ignore him as well.

5. If.....

If I could have anything in the whole world, I would choose something that wouldn't cost a penny, something that loads of people have, but not something I can get.

If I could have anything I would have a cuddle.

If I could have an hour to do exactly as I pleased I would make everyone who's made me suffer go through exactly the same kind of thing I've gone through.

If I could do anything in an hour I'd get my revenge.

If I could have one feeling only for the rest of my life, I would choose something that I don't feel anymore and something that I can't remember very well.

If I could have one feeling for the rest of my life I would choose to be happy, I would choose happiness.

6. Alone

Alone, no one to talk to with my problems
No one to turn to when I'm upset and hurt

Alone, no one to laugh with or be silly with
No one around to share the joke with

Alone, no one to argue with when I know I'm right
No one to be able to prove wrong

Alone, no one to cuddle when it's cold
No one that I can call a friend

Alone, no one to trust with any secrets
No one knows about some of the things I hide

Alone, no one to support me when I'm scared to death
No one to comfort me when people put eggs through the window

Alone, alone to face all problems on my own
Alone because apparently I deserve it

Alone just because I'm different
Alone I may be, but at least I'm more free.

7. Crying

I sit on my bed, thinking about how bad my life is and how everyone says they hate me and how they wish I would just die.

I sit on my bed and it makes me feel like crying.

I sit on my bed, wondering about what's going to happen next, am I going to die? Is somebody going to beat me again, I just think about the mess I'm in.

I sit on my bed and it makes me feel like crying.

I sit on my bed, hoping that it would all go away by the next morning and that I won't feel as rejected and lonely and left out.

I sit on my bed and it makes me feel like crying.

I sit on my bed, thinking about what will happen when my family and other people find out about me, I think about what their reaction will be.

I sit on my bed and it makes me feel like crying.

I sit on my bed thinking about everything that has happened and I notice that I've made myself too tough.

So even if I wanted to, I couldn't do any crying.

8. I Can't Remember

I can't remember what it's like to be really, really happy
I can't even remember what it's like to smile anymore.

I can't remember how to act around other people without feeling shy and awkward
I can't even remember what sort of things people say to each other.

I can't remember the last time I laughed or had a smile on my face, so it's no wonder I don't
remember what it's like to do them.

I can't remember the last time somebody was able to have a proper conversation with me as I
don't feel I can talk as freely as I used to.

I can't remember the last time I enjoyed school.
I can't remember how to join in with other groups in drama lessons.

I can't even remember what it's like to be able to act.
I can't even remember when I last did any acting at all and actually put any effort in.

The one thing I remember is how it feels to be lonely.

9. The World

The world seems a lonely place with it's grey skies and deep black seas.

The world seems to be forbidding and gloomy with the early nights and dark mornings.

The world seems to be evil with all the murders and violence and crime.

The world seems to belong to the devil with all the hate and the death and rules.

The world seems to be afraid of difference with all the racism and queer bashing.

The world seems to be occupied by only heterosexuals with all the punishment and words for homosexuals.

The world seems to be lost in a time of it's own with all it's old fashioned customs.

The world seems to be a place of unhappiness with all the fun and games going on and me not being able to join in.

The world seems to be a place of anger with all the thunderstorms and rough seas.

The world doesn't seem to want me, I'm here all alone all day every day.

The world seems to just turn and turn every day passing. Every minute, every hour, just ticking away.

The world seems to hate me and me alone, no chance to live a proper life, no one to care about me for a change, instead of leaving me to die slowly in the corner.

The world seems to be stuck in time with people not wanting things to change.

The world seems to be full of cowards not wanting to face up to problems and sort their lives out.

But the world must have some good in it somewhere. There must be someone that cares. I know that not all seas are dark and grey. Some are blue. I know it's true.

10. Missing Days

I miss the days when life was easy and free
When everything seemed to be smiling, smiling just like me

I miss the times when people would knock at the door
I would go out, get filthy and never be bored

I miss the days when it wasn't just me here
I would have someone to talk to and wouldn't need any tears

I miss the days when my life wasn't a muddle
Everything was simple and I would even get the odd cuddle

I miss the days when the moon shone brightly
The stars shone in the sky ever so slightly

I can't bare to think I won't have days like this again
I don't want to start my life all over again

11. Distant Dreams

You think about going to places far away
Places where no one can hurt you
Somewhere where the sun always shines
And the sea stays forever blue
You wake up and realise it's just another distant dream

You look at the night sky and see the moon and the stars glittering brightly.
You think what it would be like to visit them
To visit the planets in the solar system
You wake up and you realise it's just another distant dream

You imagine being a top actor, famous all over the world, starring in hundreds of films and TV
shows.
Meeting loads of new people every day
Thinking about being the best actor there is
You wake up and you realise it's just another distant dream

You hope that people will forget about you being different
For people to treat you the same
To be friendly, pleasant and smiling
For your life to be normal again
You wake up and you realise it's just another distant dream

12. Distant Dreams (Part 2)

You fall asleep dreaming about sunny beaches and about deep blue seas
Golden sunshine lasting forever
You wake and and you realise it's just another distant dream

You wonder what it's like to live a normal life
To get married like you should do
To have kids like a straight person
You wake up and you realise it's just another distant dream

You think about what it's like to be loved
To be cuddled by a really nice lad
Someone to tell you you're not sick and deranged
You wake up and you realise it's just another distant dream

You wish that life was easy
For you to be happy and healthy
To go about everyday life like other people
You wake up and you realise it's just another distant dream

Alot of things you want in life won't ever happen
You won't get the person you most want
You won't always be happy
You will wake up and most things will all be just another distant dream

13. Thinking Alone

Alone and miserable, wondering why nobody seems to care anymore.
Wishing that I had just kept my mouth shut, but it's too late, I've made a stupid mistake and now I'm paying for it.

Or is it the intolerance of other not being able to accept somebody who's different?
Or do they feel threatened in some way, thinking I will do them harm or give them a deadly disease?

I think harder.

Surely there must be at least one person who cares about me. Then I realise there is just one person and that person is me. Nobody else could care less if I died tomorrow.

No one would bother about a funeral, they'd just dump me in a ditch or throw me out to sea and watch the waves carry me off.

For a while my thoughts are on the friends I used to have. Wonder where they are now.
I look out of the window and see one of them laughing and joking with people they never used to like much, are they trying to prove something?
Are they saying or trying to say that they don't need to know me anymore?

They have no idea how much pain they've put me through.

I recall asking this former friend, if the rumours about me were true, would they still talk to me, their reply was "Yes"

Eventually this person found out the truth and hasn't spoken to me since. That was the last of my friends and now I've got no one.

14. The Waiting Game

Waiting, waiting for the sound of a familiar voice.
For someone to ask me if I'm feeling okay.
Hoping that the next knock on the door will be someone wanting to be around me and to talk to me for more than five minutes.

But it hardly ever happens.

Waiting, waiting for the teacher to dismiss the class.
For me to be able to get away from the pain of being in a class full of people criticising me.
Not knowing where the next dirty look or evil remark will come from.

But the days seem to last forever.

Waiting, waiting to wake up and realise it was all a dream.
For someone to bring me out of my slumber.
My life could be how it was before, happy and lively, maybe some mates will knock on the door and I'll go out as usual.

But I know it's all really happening to me.

Waiting, waiting to be able to turn the TV on and watch as many programmes as I like until I have to go to bed.
It's nearly time, time for the programme I've wanted to see for ages.
Until the announcer, just like my life, says it's cancelled.

15. Deep Down
(10 June 1999)

Every little movement, I fear
The sounds that echo, I long to stop
Living in panic and tormention
Happy happy
That sometime and anytime, the pain I feel will finally be laid to rest
For I cannot go on this way
Doubting myself, hating myself
Other people judging the person on the inside
Without really knowing who that person is

No time will be too soon for it to end
People beating me almost to death with their evil and cruel words
Every place that I go, anytime of the day
At least one person will destroy my wall of steel that I have tried to build around me

Deep down I am ashamed of what I am
I feel hate and resentment
I want to end it all but I never get enough courage to slaughter myself
To kill the pain of living
I must carry on
I have to be strong, I have to fight
But maybe putting an end to it would do me good

No longer would I feel the pain of those icy comments and words of destruction that ejaculate
from the mouths of the demons that surround me

Only time will tell if I am to suffer for the rest of my life
I fear for the future, for what it may bring
Disease, prejudice and the plain fact of knowing that I am seen to be a total freak of nature

Not having a soul speak one single kind word is one of the most devastating feelings that any
person will ever encounter
You feel so much rejection, you feel cold
Your emotions mix up and you don't know, after a while, who you really are

I believe that everyone needs at least one person to show forgiveness and care

Even a few meaningless words to one person might mean a lot of good feeling to another in need

Everyone gets along with each other except me
I have been thrown into my grave before I am even dead
But in a way, the person inside has already met his death
His body is just carrying him through life until he retires from Earth

I cannot imagine how I will end
But if my life so far is anything to go by, I will meet an evil, cruel and painful death

I do not care what people think or do
But I do want it to end before I lose what sanity I still possess

16. My Life

My life is like a lump of coal

Dull, black and worthless

My life is like a used tissue

Useless, screwed up and damp

My life is like a field of grass

Plain, flat and muddy

My life is like an empty can

Nothing in it and out of breath

My life is the BBC

Boring Bloody Crap

My life is like dog turd

It's dirty and it stinks

My life is like Channel Five

Pointless and pathetic

17. What Do You Do

When your life sucks
What do you do?

You forget about the crap

When you're a dirty little bastard
What do you do?

You love every minute of it

When you're feeling like total shit
What do you do?

You tell the bastards that make you feel like shit to "Fuck off you tossing bastards"

18. Boys!
(25 May 1999)

With their lovely eyes
Gorgeous smiles
Firm backsides
How can anyone resist

Boys! Boys! Boys!
They're so lovely and gorgeous
Boys! Boys! Boys!
The best damn thing in the whole wide world

It's not just boys and girls
Girls don't rule the world
Boys are the best thing on Earth
Shout these words out loud

Boys! Boys! Boys!
They're so lovely and gorgeous
Boys! Boys! Boys!
The best damn thing in the whole wide world

Boys? Yes
Girls? No way

Boys! Boys! Boys!
They're so lovely and gorgeous
Boys! Boys! Boys!
The best damn thing in the whole wide world

With their tender touch
They are strong enough

Boys! Boys! Boys!

19. Paul Mansell
(11 June 1999)

Looks so fine
Wish he was mine
Wanna hold him
But I'll never get a chance
Everytime I see him
I go into a trance

And his name?

Paul Mansell
So gorgeous, really fit
I don't know him
But I love him to bits

He walks into a room
I have to turn away
I need to stop this soon
Ooops, it's happened again
I can't help it, with his beautiful eyes
His gorgeous smile

And his name?

Paul Mansell
So gorgeous, really fit
I don't know him
But I love him to bits

Paul Mansell
So gorgeous
Really handsome
It's madness

I need to get over it, it's so pathetic
I shouldn't feel like this
But I can't help it
He's got a sexy voice

I don't know why
It's not a matter of choice

And his name?

Paul Mansell
So gorgeous, really fit
I don't know him
But I love him to bits

Will I ever stop feeling the way that I'm feeling?

What's the point of lying to myself
I know I can't help it, if I really like someone

Everything about him's fine
Everything about him's fine

Paul Mansell
So gorgeous, really fit
I don't know him
But I love him to bits

Don't know him
But he's really fit

20. Lonely Scum
(21 June 1999)

What's it like to be total scum?
I already know the answer

What's it like to be total scum?
The answer is painful and even more painful

What's it like to be total scum?
It's worse than being just scum

What's it like to be total scum?
It's like you're trapped with no way out

What's it like to be alone?
It's like a knife stabbing into you

What's it like to be alone?
You end up hating yourself more and more

What's it like to be alone?
It seems like nobody cares

What's it like to be alone?
It's the worst thing in the world

21. Painful Death

(10 & 11 June 1999)

On and on through every day
Travelling in different directions
Moving from place to place

Comments thrown and comments kept
Words that hurt and words ignored

Feeling so low, never high
Always the opposite of what I want to be

Never win, always lose
Never smile always frown
Never happy, forever sad

Need to have the courage
But can never find it
Need to fight back
Instead of turning away

No more life
Just painful death

22. What I Think Of You Really
(28 March 2000)

You'd freak if you knew I was checkin' you out
Can't help it, I'm always checkin' you out
You think I'm a freak, a useless piece of shit
Not normal you say

You're always skittin' and dissin'
Puttin' me down to the ground
You make me feel like dirt

What does it matter anyway
Why can't you just be gay
Especially if it's the only way I know how to be

When you're laughin' you don't know that you're turnin' me on
Coz I wouldn't admit it

If you were mine I wouldn't ever lie
I'd always be honest I wouldn't be as much hassle as one of your girls

Well what the fuck are you playin' at
Treatin' me like that
You little twat
Fucked up in the head
That's what you say about me
Can't do a pissin' thing right
Only come out at night

You're a fucked up prick of a dickhead
Wouldn't say it normally
But you've pushed me too far

23. Beautiful World
(9 November 1999)

Open the door, go outside
Don't be afraid, don't hide away
Clear your mind
Take a look around
You'll realise that it's a beautiful world

Forget about all the people who put you down
Pretend they're all in a book
Put it back on the shelf

Avoid things that will hurt you
Set yourself free, do what you want
Be who you want to be
Not what they want you to

Whilst you're outside take a good look at everything around you
Remember, forget about the bad stuff from the past
Don't be afraid to wander and explore
If you do this
You'll realise that it's a beautiful world

If people get in your way
Push them aside, they're useless

Those who let you be free
Keep hold of them for as long as possible
Because in the end you may need them
When it all goes wrong

Follow your dreams, even if you know you'll fail
At least you can say you've tried
When a lot of the people you know didn't

Remember that the world is a huge place
Remember that you are free to do what you want
Remember that everyone who tries to stop you is useless

The world that we live in
The world as we know it
Even though not all of it is perfect
It's still a beautiful world

This is your world
Don't be afraid and hide away from it
Don't be afraid of this beautiful world

www.ingramcontent.com/pod-product-compliance
Lightning Source LLC
Chambersburg PA
CBHW071320280526
45788CB00004B/1962